TIRED

CHURCH

MEMBERS

How To Overcome Your Church Fatigue
And Manifest In Life.

IKWUAGWU IGWE KALU

TIRED CHURCH MEMBERS

HOW TO OVERCOME YOUR CHURCH FATIGUE AND MANIFEST IN LIFE.

OTHER TITLES BY
IKWUAGWU IGWE KALU

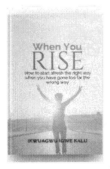

OTHER TITLES BY
IKWUAGWU IGWE KALU

OTHER BOOKS WRITTEN BY IKWUAGWU IGWE KALU

1. Tired Church Members

2. Build Not Chase

3. Fear Is An Idiot

4. When You Rise

5. 20 Positive Affirmations For Your Wealth, Health, Growth And Spirituality

6. Bahd New Year Resolutions

7. Switch

8. Affirmations For 2023

9. Hadassah: The Story Of Time

10. Post Covid-19 Church

11. Hold On, God Has Not Changed His Mind

12. Internetscape Architect

13. Get That Feedback

14. Creating Compelling Solutions To Compelling Needs

15. The 7 Letters Of Purpose

COPYRIGHT PAGE

Table of Contents

DEDICATION

To anyone who dares to be curious about their purpose, uniqueness and potential, you will redeem every lost time.

ACKNOWLEDGEMENT

People often ask me, "How do you do everything you do? How do you juggle your ministry with your purpose, business, family, profession, etc...? I often respond by saying it is the grace of God but thinking about it more, I realise it is the grace of God working through the people God has brought my way by divine arrangement.

On this note, I won't fail to mention the immense contribution the following people have made in my life and the production of this book.

My 'Chica Bonita' Amarachi has always stayed beside me, encouraging and challenging me to do more.

Charis and Nachi, my children, helped me choose the book cover design.

My pastor, Pastor Abu Jibril, I have never seen a more hardworking Pastor than he is, with results to show for it.

Kelechi Ekeghe, my padi, is always my sounding board to test some of my ideas, including this book.

The list goes on and on, but from the depth of my heart, I am grateful to everyone I have come across to find myself and serve the world through my gifts. This book is another expression of the gift you have helped me find.

Finally, I won't fail to thank My Lord God almighty, who keeps giving me the chance to live and to make an impact. Thank you.

Ikwuagwu Igwe Kalu

10th November, 2023.

Abuja.

FOREWORD

Many Christians are ashamed to admit that they are exhausted from their religious engagement with church and church people.

This book will completely change how you experience God, the church and life. It's both shock therapy and healing balm for those who are worn out and disenchanted with their church family. If you want to truly break free and appreciate the beautiful life Christ promised us, this book is for you.

You will learn why you are tired, How to take back your life and what is on the other side of your Christian experience.

Kelechi Ekeghe

General Manager Sales and Operations, CEVA Software LTD

Introduction

INTRODUCTION

You always remember the first time.

Mine came like "BOOM!" That surprising bang when it hits you for the first time with a new experience that immediately resonates with your inner happiness. I welcomed it with a grin, but my heart was ecstatic with joy that I had finally found what I could identify and run with. Everything just felt perfect.

It was the first time I heard the word 'multipotentiality'. It was in a virtual meeting in 2020 during the COVID-19 lockdown. A comment that stoked the embers of my curiosity to explore more on my potential. This was the same period I had started writing the book 'When You Rise', and the foundation of this book was laid in my heart.

According to Wikipedia, multipotentiality is an educational and psychological term referring to the ability and preference of a person, particularly one of intense intellectual or artistic curiosity, to excel in two or more different fields.

It can also refer to an individual whose interests span multiple fields or areas rather than being strong in just one. Such traits are called multipotentialities, while "multipotentialites" have been suggested as a name for those with this trait.

Christians, especially church members, are also multipotentialites. Sadly, the majority have not been allowed to explore these options beyond the four walls of the church. They have been secluded within the church to shine within and not without.

I remember the words of Jesus: "You are the light of the world." "No man lights a candle and puts it under the bucket, but he puts it on a stool to give light to everyone in the house".

Church members are the light of the world, not the light of the church, but we have repeatedly conditioned our church members to be the light of our Churches. We have frequently kept church members under the bucket, refusing their light to beam and illuminate the world. This practice has produced a lot of tired church members.

A tired church member is one whose multi potentials are not given the room to explore from within the four walls of the church to provide light to the world around us.

Presently, we face the problem of having people come to church with no sense of satisfaction because what gives them joy is not being addressed but suppressed.

Church members are meant for the world. In as much as the world is cruel and dark, they cannot avoid it. The tares have been planted beside Christians to choke them, but we can stop the tares even more; instead, we are hiding within the church, which we think is safe and comfortable.

This book explores what makes you unique and why you have been tired of the church for a long time.

It has also provided a road map to help you manifest beyond the four walls of the church, and a guide to help church leaders create a system to unbundle tiredness among church members.

This is a must-read, and I thank you for picking up this book today.

Welcome to your new manifestation!

Chapter One

1. Commentators And Players

At the time I was writing this chapter, I looked up the ten best football commentators in the world, and I saw the likes of Matin Tyler, Peter Drury, Jim Beglin, and Alan Smith. These guys will make you love the beautiful game of football matches. You could listen to their commentary on the radio, and it's as if you are watching the game live on TV or physically in the stadium.

However, one thing familiar with all of them is their inability to join the players in the game. They can only watch from afar. They will always have something to say about the players, including the coaches, but they will never get involved with the play.

The commentary doesn't affect the game's outcome because the players barely notice them. The players can only hear them if they eventually watch the match recap. All the commentators do is talk. They talk about what is going on in the field of play. They talk about who is winning and who is losing. They talk about what is going on in the area.

The field

Talking about the field brings us to one of Jesus' parables in Mathew 13:24-30; 36-43, and he referred to the field as the world and highlighted that God has planted us in the world. He didn't say that God has planted us in the church.

In the parable, Jesus also told how the enemy came by night and planted tares (weeds). The tares represent the children of the world in that parable.

At that point, the logical thing to do, as pointed out by the servants in that parable, was to uproot the tares to give room for the children of God to grow, but they were asked not to but allow both the wheat and the tares to grow together until the time of the harvest. The difference will be so clear from their fruits at harvest time.

You've been planted.

The critical thing to note from Jesus' interpretation of this parable to his disciples is that God planted you in the world. God is not worried that the world is planted beside you, so He is confident of the result coming from His children at the end of time.

The church will continue to breed tired church members when she continues to keep her members within the four walls of the church

The Church of Jesus Christ is a brand on her own while you, as a Christian, are also a brand in the world, likewise the children of the world. God has planted you in the world and commissioned you to dominate in your field as much as tares surround you. Remember, you are the light of the world. You are a city set on a hill and cannot be hidden. Men are expected to see your good works and glorify your father, who is in heaven.

The church is your home, family, and place of refuge and recharge, but you can't be home forever. Wars are not won at home because the damage will be too costly; wars are preferred to be fought and won on neutral ground far from home, where the collateral damage will be low.

Where is the problem?

Your problem is not with your church but with yourself. Your anger should not be with your church but yourself for not living up to your potential. You have chosen the easy way out to throw the blame on how you feel about the operations of your church. You are responsible for dominating your field and not your church. There's nothing to conquer within the church; all your foes are outside. Your competition is expected with the world's children, not the church.

You become tired of the church because you are fighting within the church instead of out there 'killing' it in the world.

> *Most Christians live and behave as if their whole life begins and ends in the Church.*

The church will continue to breed tired members as long as she keeps them within the four walls of the church, afraid that if they shine outside, they will be lost. The church's role is to raise disciples who will be guiding lights in the world and not be influenced or led astray. Our churches are over-saturated with too much potential lying dormant.

Do you think that if the church throws its weight behind those who understand their assignment, they won't do better or become more prominent influencers in different sectors of the world than the children of the world? Especially in the entertainment industry.

Who owns the gift?

You must own your gift, assignment, and identity as a Christian. Being a church member is an illusion; God will not ask you that on judgment day; he wants to see your fruits on the day of the harvest, or will you be mistaken for the tares?

The Wheat vs. the tares

Differentiating between the two is a daunting task. Before bearing fruit, wheat and tares bear a striking resemblance. Both plants develop side by side in the spring, but the tares outgrow the wheat, covering it with their sprawling branches, hindering its growth and ripening. As a result, the tares appear taller, sturdier, and healthier than wheat.

The seeds of wheat are weighty and abundant, bearing a stark contrast to their fully grown form. They sway with the wind's gentle touch. Thus, when the wheat reaches its

Your major concern as a Christian should be in the results you are producing and not how you feel your church is treating you.

peak and is ready for harvesting, it bends following the wind's direction. The difference is in the results.

The results are essential.

Your primary concern as a Christian should be in the results you produce, not how you feel your church is treating you. Whether Church or no church, you are responsible for living as a significant contributor to life's advancement here.

Most Christians live and behave like their whole life begins and ends in the Church. This is why your relevance doesn't go or grow beyond the four walls of the church. This is like the man who buried his talent in the ground, waiting for his master to return. We have buried many skills within the church for far too long.

You cannot afford to be a tired church member; your place is among the stars. Among the stars, laziness is not accommodated. You must work hard to earn your place.

Work for your spot.

When the wheat and tares grow together, the tares work hard to overshadow the wheat. The tares appear more robust and healthier. It would be best to work on your brand and take things into account. The world does not understand your speaking in tongues. Your speaking in tongues is between you and God, not between you and man. The world understands what they can see, hear, taste, feel and smell; what are you producing in these forms?

> *Being a church member is an illusion. Get out there and live!*

The field is the world. The good seed is the children of the kingdom. If the field is the world, and the good seed is the children of the kingdom, God is not afraid to push you into the world, and you should not be scared to live in the world.

What now here?

Thrive here.

Succeed here.

Prosper here.

God is not afraid to plant you here. He knows your breaking point, and he's not going to put you anywhere you're not going to thrive or be fruitful or successful. It doesn't make sense that the wicked succeed in the field where God has planted the believer to prosper. God assigned you to a local church to grow; He gave you to be equipped in the church to go into the world and flourish.

You have been a commentator for far too long; it's time you get on the field and play.

When you play, you play with the tares and fellow wheat, but know this: it will take work. The tares will try to overshadow and choke you, but you must stand your ground and not get tired. The church is your training ground to play in the field.

Being a church member is an illusion. Get out there and live!

Chapter Two

2. PRIESTS AND KINGS

It was mid-day towards the end of summer that year in Beer-Sheba. Winter was fast approaching, and everyone looked forward to it.

The heat that year had particularly become unbearable, so the thought of the winter cold was welcomed.

Joel was about to head out to the water room to quench his taste when Abiah, his younger brother, walked in with a bag of gold. He smiled at his brother and nodded, signalling the deal had been settled.

Both brothers were the presiding judges over the people of Israel then. They had taken over from their father, Samuel, a prophet, priest and judge of Israel.

A court session was ongoing, and the two brothers had just taken a break only to return, and Joel delivered his final judgment on the matter at hand. The land was to go to Naboth's father, the wealthy merchant of Beer-Sheba.

Welcome to Beer-Sheba

Beer-Sheba, known for its hot and dry conditions, is located in the southern part of Israel, present-day Negev in Israel. The city was witnessing at that time their worst experience with judges. It was an open denial of justice by the sons of Samuel the prophet. Justice was seen to go to the highest bidder.

Very early the next day, the elders of Israel journeyed to Ramah, demanding an audience with Samuel the prophet.

"Give us a king" they demanded.

"We have seen how kings rule with authority and no prejudice. This is the type of leadership we want since you will not be with us forever".

"We want a king who will own it all and not be biased or influenced with lucre."

This was the genesis of Kingship in Israel, scripture reference in 1Samual 8:1-22.

This was the beginning of kingship in Israel.

Man had locked himself up in the temple, and the people were not finding justice.

So there were Priests and Kings.

Before the priest was first introduced to us in the scriptures in Exodus 40:15, we had the patriarchs performing that role but for their households. At this point, the role of the priest had to be expanded because the nation of Israel (a symbol of the Church) was about to be born.

The priest's function had to encompass a more extensive coverage beyond the households but the entire nation.

As the nation evolved, having a king became imminent.

At this point, being confined within the four walls of the temple was no longer sufficient to move the nation forward.

The world community was evolving, and relationships had to be formed with other nations if Israel had to win the world over to the love of God.

The plan all along

Unknown to us, God's divine plan unfolded throughout history until the Immaculate Conception and Jesus came on the scene.

Jesus's appearance was a fusion of the priest and the king. This fusion ushered the believer into these two roles of being a priest and a king simultaneously.

> *It is the absence of this function that breeds tiredness in our roles as Church members.*

The absence of this function breeds tiredness in our roles as Church members.

Man and mystery

Man, being a lover of the mystic, is found to be naturally inclined to what appears to be mysterious. So, we naturally navigated more towards our role as priests, and fortunately, this role is more relevant in the temple. Hence, so many of us are struggling to shine within the temple. In contrast, we are called to function in the temple as priests and as kings without the temple.

It is this misrepresentation that has produced the tiredness that we see rampant today.

Revelation 5:10 (KJV)

...and hast made us unto our God kings and priests: and we shall reign on the earth.

Our role is to reign on earth while we are here; it is by no means to reign in the Church.

Even before Church

You have been commissioned to dominate even before the word church was mentioned. When you were still an idea in God's mind, it was an idea of you conquering the world and not inside the temple.

God dominates within the Church, and we all minister to Him. We all serve the Lord God in our role as a priest.

We are not a King to God but to the world and her different expressions.

> *Whereas we are called to function both in the temple as priests and as kings without the temple.*

When you begin to dwell in the Church, relegating your role as a king, you will become tired.

Where is Purpose expressed?

Your purpose in life is expressed in your kingly roles. Your goal is simply what you are built to do in this world. That agreement you had with God even as you were formed in your mother's womb. That agreement you had with your maker on your assignment in the world.

Initially, your purpose had nothing to do with church; it had everything to do with the world. In the beginning, God created the heavens and the earth, and he (God) put you here to tend to this earth.

While man tended to this earth, he became creative to solve his daily challenges. This creativity has spiralled into our present-day level of technology, economy, systems, structures and cultures.

> *The moment you begin to dwell in the Church, relegating your role as a king, you will become tired.*

The earth was perfect with profound potential. The Church came as a remedy,

Why should you continue to strive in a singular role of priesthood while you have an untapped part of kingship?

Your Purpose is unique.

God has already carved a perfect role for you with your unique purpose. It would be best to allow it to be expressed in the right environment. You have become short-sighted, thinking and hoping you will find fulfilment within the temple.

You have been in the temple for far too long. It is time to explore your bi-role of kingship.

The church doesn't need tired members but firebrand kings leading the earth. The world is yet to see innovations until kings arise and command their different domains.

> *Why should you continue to strive in a singular role of priesthood while you have an untapped role of kingship?*

Stop hiding

It is your time to rise and fulfil your role of kingship.

Your purpose is begging to be explored. It is an abuse of potential when you hide within the church, and the world is in darkness. You are the light of the world. You are a city set on a hill and cannot afford to be hidden from the world.

You have lit your candle and covered it with a bucket for far too long. It's time you stand and let your light shine so all may see your good works and glorify God.

This is why I have written this book.

> *The church doesn't need tired members but firebrand kings leading the earth.*

To challenge you that time is running out and your throne has been vacant for too long. You are a king, and you need to rule. The world needs you to lead.

Will you rule?

Will you rise to the challenge of leadership?

Are you going to permit yourself to shine?

It's time to take away the blame from your church and beam the light on your untapped potential. This is the key to unlocking the tiredness you feel within. When you find your purpose, you can live as your king.

Chapter Three

3. Motions Rhythm And Purpose

Being in the choir when I turned 18 allowed me to understand a bit about music and melodies. Mainly, I enjoy watching the instrumentalist make a gesture when they hit the right notes that are in harmony with each other. Watching them make those funny faces was fun for me. Funny, this is how I am starting this chapter on purpose.

When the instrumentalists play together, they are not after getting to a balance but after harmony. These are two different conditions. Balance is when everything is in the right proportions to achieve 100%, while harmony doesn't care so much about 100%, but it's after putting each component in its proper place not to distort the entire body's free flow.

When God created you, He agreed with your spirit on your purpose on earth. You accepted your purpose while you were still a long way from here; it was already encoded within you with ideal environments, tools and situations that it should function optimally.

This is why your unique purpose feels so good when you discover it. It is simply pure joy because it gives you this feeling of harmony that instrumentalists feel when they hit the right notes or achieve harmony with each other.

Tiredness sets in when you find yourself in a system out of tune with the rhythm of your purpose.

The circumstances and environment (location) you were born in were perfect for you to collect the necessary tools, experience, and training to fulfil your purpose. You will appreciate your journey and experience when you start with this awareness.

Sadly, many people do not fulfil their purpose while on earth because of the way our churches have been structured to keep all the talents within. This is usually a result of the fear of being corrupted when they interact with the world. Unconsciously, this mentality has been consistently transferred to church members over the years.

Stranded Church members

When a Church is structured in such a way that if you cannot function as an usher, chorister, care team member, prayer warrior, facility management (cleaners), etc., you'll be stranded, this sort of structure will always breed tired, unsatisfied and frustrated individuals and surprisingly, individuals in such situations are unaware they are already exhausted.

Where is your purpose?

Sit down quietly and ask yourself: why am I here? Sit down quietly and find out your purpose. You have a purpose; you may or may not know it yet. You can know your purpose by asking yourself and being true to yourself. One major clue is that your purpose can NEVER be that thing that does not give you joy and satisfaction.

Rhythms and purpose

Let me share this analogy with you; when you use the manual cycling machine, it simulates your physical body into making motion, and while this is going on, the body gets into a rhythm.

Any disorder to this rhythm, you'll find yourself tripping, which is a sure symptom of disorder, and chaos breeds tiredness.

Your purpose is a motion, and any disorder to the rhythm brings you to a tired state.

Your purpose is like music. It comes originally with a tune and rhythm. Tiredness sets in when you find yourself in a system out of tune with the rhythm of your purpose.

There are lots of tired people in our churches today, not because they don't love Jesus. They love Jesus and want to do what pleases Him, but fatigue sets in when the purpose of the man or woman does not resonate with the man-initiated systems.

It's your responsibility to find this.

It is not ordinary to find out you are tired and fed up. It's

> *The surest way to enjoy your church membership is to function within your purpose in life.*

not because Church in her purest form is faulty but that the unique core of your being is not being allowed to find expression.

It is your duty and responsibility to find and give yourself that expression. When you delegate this role, you mismanage your expectations from the Church. Every expectation and emotion ought to be managed. You can't afford to throw your emotions and expectations carelessly out there. When you do, chances are you are going to get heartbroken.

Imagine being in love; you can't help but have certain expectations from your lover, but even in this enchanted state, room should be left to manage these emotions and expectations.

The surest way to enjoy your church membership is to function within your purpose in life. Work and function within your purpose in life. Not what you've been forced into or available based on the knowledge available to the church at that time. Go ahead and do what you know you've been called from within.

You will always be energised when you function within your purpose.

Beyond the traditional ministries

Churches that create ministries beyond the traditional choir, ushering, technical, media, prayer, care team, etc. units will always have less tired church members. Ministries include politics and governance, community service, academic excellence among teenagers, campaigns against drug usage among teenagers, etc. The list goes on and on, but the important thing is that you create ministries that solve societal problems.

> *You will never be tired when you function within your purpose.*

What is that unique solution?

One thing familiar with every purpose is that purpose is unique, and it invariably solves a unique problem. Create opportunities where church members can plug in their unique purposes, and you will find individuals who will burn for Jesus and never become tired.

Let's go beyond our traditional thinking of keeping all and sundry within the four walls of the Church. We are not called to be within the church, and just like the dove Noah sent out, we can't be locked up within the ark forever.

Chapter Four

4. Adjectives vs. Nouns

Growing up, it was easy to grab a name tag either in mockery, admiration or acknowledgement of your special abilities. Such names or tags have a way of describing you. This is what an adjective does to a noun.

A noun is the name of a person, place or thing.

An adjective describes a noun.

When a man says he is a doctor, he must prove it with his results.

It is the result that describes him as a doctor. Likewise, your results as a Christian describe who you are. When you start seeing the word "Christian" not as a badge or title but as a name that needs to be proven, you start living up to the name.

Welcome to Antakya

In the city of Antioch, which is present-day Antakya in Turkey. Antioch held such a significant place in the heart of the epistles found in the New Testament Bible. It was a vantage point for the apostles to reach the Gentiles. The book of Acts describes that at Antioch, the apostles did much teaching, which produced an identity that has stuck with us till today.

It was in Antioch that believers of Jesus Christ were first called Christians. This was in a description of who they were and who they represented.

Our churches today are rooms filled with so much light that no one wants to go out there in the dark.

It wasn't a mere name to give them as an identity but an adjective that described who they were.

Today, the word 'Christian' continues to describe who we are. The question remains: are we living up to that description?

Results vs. identity

Jesus produced results, and his disciples followed suit after his ascension. The believers produced similar results to Jesus, so they were described as 'Christians'.

Today, we have taken the word 'Christian' as an identity, not a description. When it is an identity, no work is required; there are no good works to show before men so they can glorify God. As a description, then works and results must follow.

> *What breeds tiredness among church members is shining light fatigue called photophobia.*

Shining in the dark

Our churches today are rooms filled with so much light that no one wants to go out there in the dark. This is what lighting a candle and putting it under the bucket means. You cannot give light to everyone in the house this way. The world is dying because we are not shining,

Beyond the walls

There is too much light in our church halls. God is already in our midst because where 2 or 3 are gathered in his name, He is present and our light. This means that our light is not needed inside the church halls but in the different sectors of the world.

You cannot be a Christian inside the church walls; you are a Christian because you are manifesting beyond the four walls of the church. Antioch was a pagan city then, so it was apparent to identify the believers when they stepped into town. No one would have described them as Christians if they were locked up within the temple or stayed back in Jerusalem.

Photophobia syndrome

What breeds tiredness among church members is shining light fatigue called photophobia. One of the medical effects of photophobia is fatigue, nausea and head pain. Spiritually, we have likewise induced our spirit man with too much light, causing fatigue, nausea and head pain among church members.

The world isn't saturated yet; the church is flooded with light. It's time we let people out of the four walls of the church. It is time we make the teachings in church applicable to our everyday life from Monday to Saturday. This has to be an intentional act.

Our Sunday sermons should apply in boardroom meetings, business negotiations, and football matches, as we attend to clients and give an injection in the emergency unit. Everywhere, the light of God's word should saturate the world. It is a lack of expression beyond the four walls of the church that breeds tiredness among church members.

Tiredness produces frustration over time.

We have trained our choristers to sing well and stir up the anointing, but we have yet to emphasise why they should be exceptional secretaries in the public space. Could this be why we have only a few Christians as influencers worldwide? We have allowed the world to define influence for us while we are busy dragging the stage within the church.

> *It is a lack of expression beyond the four walls of the church that breeds tiredness among church members.*

Chapter Five

5. Expressions And Suppressions

C atharsis is a term used in psychology and literature to describe releasing or purging strong emotions, often through artistic or emotional expression. The concept of catharsis originates in ancient Greek philosophy, particularly in the works of Aristotle.

In psychology and emotional contexts, catharsis refers to releasing pent-up emotions or tension, which can be therapeutic and provide emotional relief. The idea is that by expressing and experiencing intense emotions, such as sadness, anger, or fear, in a controlled and constructive manner, individuals can alleviate emotional stress and find a sense of closure or resolution.

Expressions

Catharsis can occur through various means, including crying, talking and sharing, physical activities, artistic expression and therapeutic techniques. The bottom line is the word **release** or **expression.** Emotions must be expressed or released and not suppressed or bottled up, which is what this chapter is about.

> *Emotions have to be expressed or released and not suppressed or bottled up*

Our churches today have barely made room for catharsis; we have only provided limited options, and these options tend to crucify and resurrect overnight instead of allowing for at least three days in the grave to deal with the darkness. Let me explain, for example, for matters that deal with human emotions like divorce, loss of a livelihood, loss of a loved one, etc., we tend to push individuals into acts such as forgiveness, forgetting the past and moving on, instead of taking them through the process of these acts.

In the process of these acts, the individual can find catharsis to express these emotions in a manner that can foster healing and authentic expression. Our gathering should be a safe space for expression that brings healing. When missing, it brings and encourages tiredness within our coming together.

The need for updated ministries

It is important to note that our usual rituals of orthodox confessions, sacraments and congregational hymns will not provide a deep and adequate catharsis in this present age. We must offer ministries that will engage our purposes in life and not our traditional ministries that focus mainly inward.

Historically, Churches have relied on confessions and rituals for catharsis.

The need to belong

When you belong to a denomination, family, workplace, or community, you can't help but find different, unique emotions at play from other individuals.

This is why communities are formed and why you belong to different communities or strive to belong to certain communities and societies. You want to give your emotions some expression.

Suppression always tends to backfire

Ask a man who wants to break away from a particular habit or indulgence; you will find out that suppression is the worst strategy to apply.

Suppression breeds tiredness and frustration, while expression breeds life.

Our gathering should be a safe space for expression that brings healing.

When you find yourself in a place where your emotions are suppressed, it's a sign that you must manage or change that location.

The illusion of expression

What you find in our denominations today is 'the illusion of expression.'

You are given a platform in a local body to express yourself only within the body and never outside the body.

This also is suppression.

Religion has been crafted to suppress your emotions and left you to find a way around it to give yourself that needed expression.

Tired church members are those whose emotions have been suppressed instead of being allowed to express themselves within and beyond the walls.

Here's how to find this expression that will cure your church fatigue, or if you are a church leader and have tired members, here's what you can do as well.

Ezra's Narrative

Here's Ezra's narrative that helps us look deeper into catharsis. When Israel began the construction of the Second Temple, as everyone shouted and praised God, the elders who witnessed the temple's former glory wept uncontrollably, their wails blending in with the joyful noise (Ezra 3:12-13).

Reading this account leaves one reeling with emotion. The people who returned to their land, laden with the weight of past glory and destruction, are now rebuilding their temple. After suppressing their emotions for 50 years, they finally have a chance to release them. One can only imagine the messiness and the liberating feeling of letting it all out.

Tired church members are those whose emotions have been suppressed instead of being allowed to express themselves not just within the walls but beyond the walls.

It's a community.

However, what astounds me the most is that this catharsis isn't an individual experience. It is shared with the community, an integral part of their communal life. There is no rebuke from the storyteller or hint that it is unusual. It is accepted as part of their culture.

Are we shy?

Contrast that with our current church culture, which shies away from such displays of emotion. In our pursuit of freedom, we neglect to acknowledge and give space for long-held emotions to be released. Our churches, often dealing with topics that evoke strong emotions, are not equipped to handle such outbursts. Imagine if someone in your congregation broke down on a Sunday, their cries loud enough to be mistaken for shouting. How would we respond? What would we say about them?

As a community, we struggle to navigate and make room for big emotions despite constantly being surrounded by situations that stir them. We must learn to embrace and acknowledge the role of emotions in our communal journey to continue to succeed at creating a safe space for healing and growth.

Healing by catharsis

When faced with crises such as pandemics, pastoral abuses, or failure, humanity experiences a surge of emotions. We collectively feel hurt, sadness, and anger, among other powerful sentiments. However, in our pursuit to return to normalcy, we often overlook the need for moments of communal praise, mourning, and celebration. As a result, our communities may still carry unresolved trauma, and our attempts at resurrection may not have been fully addressed past crucifixions.

Sometimes, we convince ourselves that we are fine as long as we are not shouting or expressing our emotions. We need these messy and chaotic moments to move forward and heal as a community. Because

> *In our pursuit of freedom, we neglect to acknowledge and give space for long-held emotions to be released.*

even though they may seem turbulent, they ultimately bring cleansing and liberation. And despite our silence on specific issues, they have not disappeared; we must allow ourselves the catharsis of acknowledging and releasing these pent-up emotions.

When catharsis is employed

Most church fatigues are a result of pent-up emotions looking for expression. It's possible to become a tired church member and not know it. In subsequent chapters, I will discuss the signs to look out for that indicate the fatigued church member state. This explains why, most times, we experience some relief when we change our place of worship to a place that makes room for emotional release.

Chapter Six

6. Stop Shrinking Your Vision

If you stay in an environment where people do not recognise your value as a unique person with a unique vision and purpose, you will be forced to shrink your vision and purpose to the size they can understand and handle. This is one major cause of anxiety, dissatisfaction and, ultimately, tiredness.

Depression starts from the point where you know you can do more, but you are not allowed to do more just because your environment cannot handle more. This is what a toxic relationship looks like. You need to understand that no matter how small you look, it does not make you small: you are big.

You have a big vision.

You have a big purpose.

You have a big influence.

Stop doing this to yourself.

Where both you and your environment can no longer cope, the reasonable thing to do is to part ways.

Stop limiting yourself to the size of your church building. It is not your fault that your pastor is not developing themselves to accommodate your growth; yes, it's not your fault. Every man has a responsibility to himself to grow in personal development. This is not a call to look down or dishonour your pastor but for you to know what is good for you and maintain your conversation and not compromise it.

There is a thin line between recognising your value as a human being and being arrogant with this awareness. It is a thin line because it's easy to become arrogant with this knowledge and disrespect and dishonour authority. With your awareness of who you are and the assignment you've been called to carry out comes a heavy responsibility to become accountable with such awareness. Failure with this responsibility always leads to shame, ridicule and total failure.

Carry others along

No matter how successful you are, if those around you are not growing with you, they will find a way to bring you to their level. It is easier to adjust by reduction than by increase; the former is quite convenient. When you find yourself in an environment uninterested in

Stop limiting yourself to the size of your church building.

growth and have become aware of this, wisdom demands that you do something about it by offering the same opportunities to your environment. Where both you and your environment can no longer cope, the reasonable thing to do is to part ways.

Are you tired of growth?

You become tired of growth when your environment is uninterested in embracing change. Development requires that many things change, and recently, most of our evolution has been disruptive, making many people uncomfortable. Growth is not always comfortable.

That vision is begging for your attention.

God has already given you a vision, and it doesn't matter whether you are aware of it or not; that vision is within your heart, seeking your attention. Peradventure, you've become aware of your vision; you shouldn't be laid back in pursuing it. Every vision requires that you nurture it by feeding it; this includes the environment you've provided for the vision. Your vision is like a baby; it will look like whatever you are feeding it and the environment where it is being fed.

Explore and become curious.

Explore new options and ways of doing things. As much as possible, don't get stuck in old ways even if it is working. There's no growth in following the status quo.

You are responsible for your purpose, vision and future; you cannot blame anybody or your church when you hit the rocks. It is solely your responsibility. Your church is a support system but not your only support. You have an inbuilt personal support system, which includes your spirit, mind and body. With these 3, there's nothing you cannot do and nothing you cannot attract.

> *You become tired of growth when your environment is not interested in embracing change.*

Stop shrinking your vision to the size of your church.

Stop shrinking your purpose to the size of your church.

Stop shrinking your future to the size of your church.

Where it starts

You will be frustrated for a long time if you keep doing this. Your church fatigue started the day you abandoned some of your ideas because your church told you 'they' don't do such things. Imagine a scenario where your church tells you not to nurture or grow your political ambition because they feel politics is a dirty game. A situation where your church tells you politics will corrupt you as the prayer machine of the church, or your political career will cause them to lose you as their drummer.

It would be best if you had an alignment.

Don't put your life, vision and purpose in the hands of men, especially those whose vision and future are not aligned with yours; if not, they will fit you into their vision.

Don't tailor-fit

You don't have to fit or tailor your vision to fit church style or to be like your church. The people you have been called to reach do not understand the church language. Some of them might not have heard about your church.

> *Your church fatigue started the day you abandoned some of the ideas you've got because your church told you 'they' don't do such things.*

A good product is designed to serve the customers' needs and location. Similarly, your vision should be tailored to serve the needs and location of those it is meant for. It is your responsibility to do this.

Go all out and fight for your vision. Fight and give it space to breathe. Your vision is your baby. Do not prevent it from growing because you feel the growth might not be accepted, but instead, go where it is accepted and thrive there.

Emotional blackmail

At first, we become emotionally attached to our churches because we have made friends, fostered business partnerships and deepened some bonds. When it's time to leave, your emotions begin to blackmail you. If you need to leave a place and don't leave, you will become tired of that place without knowing it.

> *God's call is not only for the pulpit; God calls us to the government house.*

You have become a tired church member. Maybe it's time to change your environment, but you've succumbed to the emotional blackmail and stayed back.

You can't force a vision to thrive in a place not meant for that vision. This usually leads to vision abandonment, which is why many people have abandoned their visions.

Don't give in to the bad feeling.

Every vision you have deserves a chance to thrive. Getting an idea or a vision indicates the trust God has put in you to handle what he has in mind to do. Resist the urge not to hurt your relationships and not give yourself wholly to what God has called you to do. God's call is not only for the pulpit; God calls us to the government house. God's call is not limited to anywhere in this world. You will become a tired church member when you limit God's call within the four walls of the church.

Your vision is your baby. Do not prevent it from growing because you feel the growth might not be accepted but instead go where it is accepted and thrive there.

Chapter Seven

7. When Will You Ever Be Bold?

A ccording to the Book of Genesis, the creation story describes how and for what purpose you were created. God first made you unique with unique qualities and assignments. It is your number one assignment to live this unique life uniquely and enjoy it.

Your life is never about church membership. You are encouraged to belong to a denomination because that's where God-ordained ministers will teach you the word of God. God designed His word to be taught by certain people He has anointed and sent to do so. This is why it's essential to be committed to a particular body of Christians who are learning the word of God together and building a community of compassionate character and practice.

What is stopping you?

Paul was imprisoned and could no longer attend church meetings in the temple or preach in church, but this didn't stop him from living his best life. He went ahead to exercise boldness with his purpose and assignment by writing letters, which today have formed the bedrock of our faith.

Your life is never about church membership.

While you are in your tired state, what are you doing? Your time on earth is not on pause because you are tired. Your purpose is not on hold, waiting for you to feel good before starting. With each passing day, you are getting closer to the grave; are you going to die with your purpose unfulfilled?

Not a function of church membership

Your success is not a function of your church membership but the personal decision you are willing to make and stand by. Life expects a lot from you, and you must give it. There's no room for laziness and laid-back attitudes that go on to throw blame.

What's your alibi?

You are using the Church as an alibi for not succeeding, not growing, not becoming a person of excellence, and not developing your talents and gifts. Nobody or institution should be an excuse for your poor performance. The church is a human development institution. It's to develop you into being a leader within your industry.

While you are at your tired state, what are you doing? Your time on earth is not on pause because you are tired.

When you use the 144+ work hours outside of the four walls of the church, what do you produce? Those should be your best hours because this is where you take the teachings you have learned in the church and light up the world. The world should be able to say:

How are you doing this without compromising?

Why are you so happy without smoking and drinking?

How are you doing this?

God placed you here.

You have the potential to be the light anywhere you are. You are a solution looking for a problem. An answer: looking for a question. You are abundance looking for scarcity, and God placed you here. You are full of solutions and answers, and what bothers you about the world bothers God. He sent you here, and you are part of the solution to the world's pressing needs. It is you that many of us have prayed for, but you're here waiting when God is waiting on you. You are the answer to your prayer; you're the answer to someone's prayer.

What's on your mind?

Make up your mind that you must express yourself. The church is not your problem. The church is a perfect institution with clear-cut goals and assignments in your life. The rest is your responsibility, and you must live up to it. Find a way to express yourself outside of the church and still maintain your integrity because this is how men will see your good works and glorify your Father, who is in heaven.

What is your work approach?

How would you approach your job? What would you do differently? When you showed up in your workplace, what would your mentality be? Will you be asking for permission to express yourself?

You should walk in and say, "I got this solution".

Please give this solution to ensure you are in your potential. You can't give God the glory when you are not in your potential. You have to expand your capacity to give God credit. God gives answers to the world's problems through people. So why does it have to be other people? Why can't it be you?

When will you be bold?

With the way you are living, when will you ever be bold? When will you ever be proactive with your purpose and stop hiding behind your church? Your purpose should shine beyond the four walls of the church. It is the lack of use of your purpose that is making you tired, bitter and frustrated.

The world is looking for problem solvers, and you are a problem solver. We travel far to look for the best tailors, doctors, coaches, etc. Since you desire the best, why can't you aspire to be the best for

Make up your mind that you must express yourself. The church is not your problem.

someone else? Be the best other people are looking for; this is how you add value and solve problems for good.

If you expect the best from others, why would you want to lower the standard for yourself? If you're looking for the best, why can't you be what you're looking for in your industry? What's stopping you? For sure, I know it is not your church. Why do you prefer to play with mediocrity as the standard for your performance? If you're in the kingdom, you've got greatness on the inside.

Where's excellence?

Excellence should always be your explanation, and you should want to be the best. It would be best if you were the best at what you do and not compare yourself with anybody else, being the best version of yourself. The church helps us develop our human resources; the least you can do is be tired of it.

Chapter Eight

8. You Are A Leader

You are a leader. It is your choice to determine how far your leadership will help improve the lives of others around you.

A leader identifies a problem, allocates a solution, and shows that the solution is effective. A leader is someone who looks at the situation and asks the question: what needs to be done and then goes about doing it? A leader is an innovator, a leader is a trailblazer, a leader is an initiator, and they're not afraid to have their ideas challenged. A leader does not wait for things to change; he initiates the change.

A leader empowers others for greatness. A leader desires that the next generation or their legacy do more incredible things than what they did.

A leader and others

He empowers others to succeed in influencing others to do well and to do great things. He allows others to believe in their ability. A leader is not someone who has a title. It's someone who has the power, privilege, and honour and goes about that business.

By now, you would have started feeling what you should be doing with your life to fulfil the talents and time God has given you here on earth. While in it, know that you are the leader in that venture.

Not always loved

A leader is only sometimes loved and admired. Take, for example, Adolf Hitler; he was a leader that no one in this part of the world admired, but he was a leader. Leadership is not a title. Another example is Prince Charles in comparison to Lady Diana. Prince Charles had the title, while Diana had the influence.

No-nonsense

Leadership is someone with a different characteristic than a charismatic one. Many times, we think that everyone has to be charismatic, and I think about Steve Jobs; he was in your face and no-nonsense, and people didn't like him, but today, technology was pushed forward, education and everything that required technology was pushed forward, but it wasn't because he was charismatic.

An opportunity to make a difference

You lead people, and you manage things. Many people think that you manage people, but you don't do that. And so

> It is your choice to determine how far your leadership is going to help improve the lives of others around you.

when God places you in your field and industry, he's putting you there to make a difference and affect the bottom line. You do this by operating as a leader or in the office of a leader, irrespective of whether you have a title.

This should apply to your family and your community; you are not a spectator, you are not a commentator, and you are a participator. The world is looking to you to solve the problems, and that's what you should do.

Raise your standard

In Chapter One, I talked about the wheat and the tares; it was about succeeding in your field. You should raise your standard and not blame everything on the devil because he's planting his people in God's field. They are not afraid to succeed there, and neither should you.

> *You lead people and you manage things.*

You should have the revelation that this is God's earth. This is God's industry; God has planted you here, and you are carrying the solution. It would be best if you were about your father's business. You should be praying: how do you want me to contribute to this industry? This community, this nation. What solution should I be bringing to the table? What problems demand my solution?

A pull on your purpose

The command is to go into all the world, not all your country; go into all the world. Wherever God has planted you, you should thrive there, and when you get in that place, you will realise it's got a pull on your purpose and mindset, and you know that that's where you should be. With this knowledge and revelation, you must be about your father's business to hone your skills, maximise your potential, and put your best foot forward. Wherever God places you, wherever he has assigned you, you are there to succeed.

The opportunity to be the first

Adam was assigned to the Garden of Eden without education and became the first zoologist and leader. Elijah was told to go by the brook called Cherith, and

John the Revelator fulfilled his assignment on the Island of Patmos. Joseph was in Egypt; Daniel was in Babylon. Rehab was in Jericho; Gandhi was in India; Martin Luther King, Atlanta, Georgia; Winston, Churchill, London, England; Barack Obama in Washington, DC, United States of America, and I can keep going on.

You should raise your standard and not blame everything on the devil because he's planting his people in God's field.

Where has God planted you?

Where has God planted you? And wherever he has planted you? There, you should succeed.

There is a call and demand for your leadership, but you've been unavailable because you are locked up within the church.

You are unavailable because your church has not let you know any better.

You are unavailable because you are bitter with the way your church has treated you, not knowing you are hurting yourself instead.

You are unavailable because you are operating at the level of your local assembly.

Time to switch sides

It's time you switch positions and move from being a tired church member to becoming a child of God, unafraid to succeed and manifest in this world. The best place to start is here and now.

Please text me at +234 703 577 2007 or write me at ikwuagwuigwe@gmail.com to book a conversation on the next step.

Bonus Chapter

HOW TO IDENTIFY TIRED CHURCH MEMBERS

1. Those who forget what they've been taught immediately after service.

2. They sleep during the sermon but awake once the sermon is over.

3. The one who keeps blaming the church for their sore predicament in life.

4. The one who keeps on complaining about church leadership.

5. The one who is bitter about the church leadership but cannot leave because of the peanuts coming from the same leadership.

6. The one forbidden to explore their purpose while serving in the church.

7. The one who is tired of using their hard-earned money to sow uniforms for church and is indebted doing so.

8. The one who doesn't want to leave a particular denomination because they feel they have become too old to change their church.

9. The one who feels it's a sin to change their church.

10. The one who attends a church simply because of what they can get and not for what they can also give.

11. The one who finds fault with every decision or move the church makes.

13. The one who comes to church so that the pastor or the leaders will not call to ask why they didn't come.

14. The one who is afraid to ask questions.

15. The instrumentalists that don't sit during the sermon but prefer to stay outside talking.

16. The one who is more interested in taking a selfie during church service than in participating in the service.

17. The person who doesn't know that there's life beyond the four walls of the church.

18. The one who doesn't have a community outside the church.

19. The one who has been brainwashed not to study the Bible for themselves.

20. Those who come to church just to be seen that they are present.

21. Those who distract themselves during the sermon.

22. Those who pretend to be paying attention during the sermon.

23. Those who scroll through their social media handles during the sermon.

24. Those who pretend to be giving offerings while they're not.

NOTES

NOTES

ABOUT THE AUTHOR

Ikwuagwu Igwe Kalu is a practising Architect, father, businessman, and licensed and certified life coach.

His eclectic approach to a purpose-driven life embraces the need to introduce the concept and subject of purpose into our urban workplaces to achieve personal and organisational goals and targets.

He is married with two children and lives in Abuja, Nigeria.

Check him at ikwuagwuigwe.com